THEN & NOW

WORCESTER COUNTY

THEN & NOW

WORCESTER COUNTY

Robin Chandler-Miles
and Norma Miles

In memory of Tom Patton, whose dedication to the preservation of Worcester County history is unsurpassed.

ISBN 978-0-7385-8222-1

Library of Congress Control Number: 2010939083

Published by Arcadia Publishing
Charleston, South Carolina

Printed in the United States of America

For all general information, please contact Arcadia Publishing:
Telephone 843-853-2070
Fax 843-853-0044
E-mail sales@arcadiapublishing.com

Visit us on the Internet at www.arcadiapublishing.com

On the Front Cover: Merry Sherwood Plantation in Berlin was built in 1859 and has been listed on the National Register of Historic Places since 1991. Built by Mr. Henry Johnson, the Greek Revival–style home had many owners through the years and finally fell victim to neglect and the scourge of time. Merry Sherwood, lovingly restored by current owner Mr. Kirk Burbage, is one of Worcester's most brilliant gems. (Images courtesy Kirk Burbage, Art Baltrotsky.)

On the Back Cover: This picture was taken in the mid-1920s and shows the north end of Market Street in Pocomoke City. The Empire Theater, the three-story building located in the center of the picture, is advertising a production of *The Sophomore*; a small Atlantic Gasoline Station is visible at right. The Atlantic Station building has been restored and still occupies this spot. (Courtesy Costen House Museum.)

Contents

ACKNOWLEDGMENTS

We wish to thank everyone who contributed images and information to this book. As always, our Worcester County Libraries were a wonderful resource. The Julia A. Purnell Museum, Mt. Zion Church, and Ocean Pines Association generously opened their repositories to us. CR Booksellers, the Spirit of Newtown Committee, the Sturgis One-Room School Museum, and the Calvin B. Taylor Foundation shared rare images and information from Worcester County's past.

We also wish to thank Jean Allen, Ruth Bates, Beulah Baylis, Hattie Beckwith, J. Chandler, Tracy Chandler King, and Dawn Chandler Trader for photographs and information. Cynthia Burbage, Kirk Burbage, Richard Gladding, Jenny Hopkinson, Sandra Hudson, Curt Lippoldt, Chris Miles, Mabel Midgett Rogers, and Winnie Small really came through for us. Special thanks go out to George S. Bunting, the Preston Marshall family, Bill and Kate Matthews, Tom Patton, Brice Stump, Dr. Arnold Torres, Mike Queen, Mickey Wigglesworth, and the wonderful folks at the Town of Ocean City City Hall. Sherrie Beckstead and Theresa Bruner at St. Martin's Church went above and beyond, as did Robert F. Jones; he shepherded us all over Stockton and Girdletree as he recounted priceless bits of local history.

The people and businesses that assisted us in reproducing the images cannot be discounted—Amanda Mitchell at Minuteman Press, Mario Bonilla at the UPS Store, Kim Scholl at Advantage Color Labs, and the helpful folks at Snow Hill Business Center were instrumental in putting this collection together. Thanks, Salisbury Walgreens!

We owe our greatest debt of gratitude to our families and friends for their unfailing patience and support and to the people of Worcester County without whose diligence there would be no history to show and tell.

All now images throughout the book are courtesy of the authors unless otherwise noted.

Introduction

Capt. John Smith and Giovanni de Verranno explored this area in the 1600s. The city of Snow Hill was born along the Pocomoke River as early as 1642, and the county was officially formed and named for an Earl Of Worcester following a division of Somerset County in 1742. In Worcester, residents prize and preserve their history while also fully embracing growth and change. They are as proud of the galleries, museums, and schools as they are of the wild ponies and golf courses. Bordered on the northern end by Delaware and on the southern end by Virginia, Worcester County is 695 square miles of diversity.

The authors both grew up in Worcester County, where they used the county libraries, attended the fine county schools, and enjoyed the close-knit rural community life. The authors bought Dolle's Popcorn and Thrasher's French Fries on visits to Ocean City and went fishing, camping, and hiking in the counties' state parks. The seemingly endless summer days were enjoyed by slurping sun-warmed tomatoes pulled right out of the garden and taking lazy drives through county burgs named Boxiron, Germantown, and Cedar Hall. In the fall, they enjoyed the secluded paths and dazzling trees in Worcester that were heavy with apples and black walnuts and blazing with red and gold leaves of every shape and size. Winter brought oysters and the possibility of sodden snow, along with holiday parades and pageants, windows glowing in the early dark like waning fireflies, and cold, quiet nights that left windows etched with fragile lace. In the springtime, the winter coats were swapped for new spring finery in preparation for Ocean City's Easter Parade. It does not really matter that the authors grew up some 30 years apart—their experiences in Worcester County were very similar and quite wonderful.

This collection of images will allow the reader to see how places have changed in the county, for better or for worse. They represent the efforts of the farmers, scholars, and business and church people who came before and the decisions they made about their livelihoods and growth in Worcester. In some cases, devastating fires and storms forced change; in others, shifting fortunes and changing mores led the way. In the end, it is the people—those whose roots were here and those who came because they appreciated all it had to offer—who played the largest part in Worcester County's survival and successes. The same is true today.

Pocomoke City's early newspaper, the *Ledger-Enterprise,* printed these words in an article dated July 4, 1908: "Why do our young men and women leave the small villages for the cities? Because the villages are not sufficiently beautified and humanized. The great thing needed by Americans and especially rural Americans, is to learn how to live. We know how to make money, how to conduct schools and how to vote, but we have not yet divined the secret of gladness, companionship, appreciation and beauty that may be extracted from life. Make the farm and village attractive. Develop the community life, the artistic, the love of beautiful—in a word, learn how to live."

CHAPTER

AT HOME IN WORCESTER COUNTY

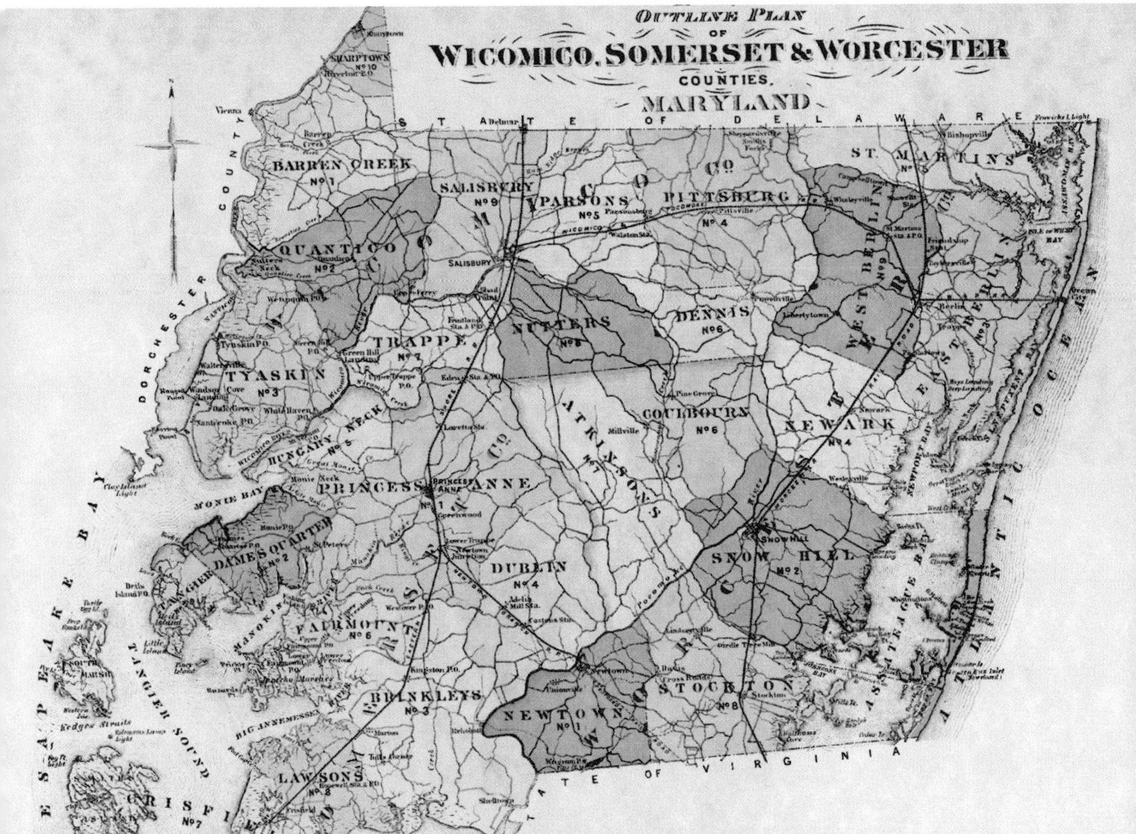

The Algonquin Indians were the earliest inhabitants of the area known as Worcester County. The temperate climate, fertile soil, wide variety of wildlife, and access to the river made this a consummate choice. Charted and explored by Capt. John Smith in the 1600s, the county was carved from neighboring Somerset County in 1742. Worcester was primarily an agricultural area, but its proximity to waterways led to rapid growth. This map shows early Worcester County on the right comprised of Newtown (now called Pocomoke City), Stockton, Snow Hill, Newark, East and West Berlin, and St. Martin's. (From *Atlases and Early Maps of the Eastern Shore of Maryland, 1877.*)

The Costen House, home of Pocomoke City's first mayor, Dr. Isaac Costen, sits at 206 Market Street. Dr. Costen's medical office was also located here. The residence, built in the 1870s and considered a significant example of Italianate-influenced Victorian architecture, was rescued from demolition in 1974. The house was accurately restored and is lovingly maintained by the Spirit of Newtown Committee and now serves as a museum. Costen House was added to the National Register of Historic Places in 1975. (Both courtesy Costen House Museum, 1971.)

Pocomoke City, called Newtown until 1878, flourished thanks to the trading and traveling opportunities afforded by the Pocomoke River. By 1820, more than 150 people lived and worked in the town, and by 1877 that number had grown to 1,500. The National Register of Historic Places designated several streets in Pocomoke City as a historic district in 2004. Second Street, seen here looking south, was recognized for the late Victorian and Federal-style homes that remain on the street. Second Street is located just two blocks from the scenic Pocomoke River and steps from the town's business district. (Historical image courtesy Worcester County Library, Pocomoke Branch.)

This is a view of Walnut Street seen from Second Street. Walnut Street was also recognized as part of the historic district because of the significant architecture of many of the structures lining the quiet street. Mature trees obscure several of the homes now, but most have been lovingly maintained or restored. The *c.* 1860 house on the left, a National Register home, serves as Littleton's Bed and Breakfast Inn and features four Victorian-style guest rooms. (Historical image courtesy Worcester County Library, Pocomoke Branch.)

This stately home was built in the 800 block of Pocomoke City's Market Street in 1907. Occupied by the Hartley Stevens family for many years, the house was purchased by the local Soroptimist Club in 1953 for use as a convalescent home. The refurbished structure known as Hartley Hall served as a nursing home until 1979. Modern residences now occupy the lot where the home stood for almost 80 years. (Historical image courtesy Costen House Museum.)

Known as the Francis M. Wilson House, this beautiful brick residence at the corner of Market and Second Streets in Pocomoke City was built in the late 1920s.The original Wilson home, a stunning two-and-a-half-story house with eight columns in front, was destroyed by the fire that ravaged the downtown area in 1922. By the 1950s, the house had been torn down and a J.J. Newberry & Co. department store was built on the site. The Newberry's store moved to a new location in the late 1980s, and the building has now been altered inside to accommodate several different businesses. (Historical image courtesy Costen House Museum.)

Esham's Dairy Farm occupied a once pastoral spot on the busy Route 113 corridor in Berlin until the late 1970s. Berlin Nursing and Rehabilitation Center, a 192-bed facility, opened on this site in 1980. The 62-bed Atlantic General Hospital opened adjacent to the Berlin Nursing and Rehabilitation Center in 1993 and serves as Worcester County's only hospital. (Historical image courtesy Taylor House Museum.)

Often called the "wedding cake house" because of its graceful tiers and decorative flourishes, Berlin's Merry Sherwood was completed in 1859 and combines classic Italianate style with Greek Revival and Gothic touches. The 27-room plantation home was built by Philadelphian Henry Johnson, who met and fell in love with a Berlin girl named Elizabeth Henry. Ownership of the house changed many times through the years, and by the 1970s the lack of resources required to maintain the home resulted in its dilapidation. Local businessman Kirk Burbage acquired Merry Sherwood in 1991, and a thorough restoration of the home and surrounding property ensued. Merry Sherwood now serves as an inn and offers an opulent setting for weddings, parties, and community events. (Both images courtesy Kirk Burbage.)

Extensive work was required to repair the damage left by aging and neglect at Merry Sherwood. These images showing the southwest corner are good examples of the poor condition of the house when Burbage acquired it and the subsequent renovations. The lovingly restored property is included on the National Register of Historic Places. (Both images courtesy Kirk Burbage.)

Boise Cascade Home and Land Corp. spearheaded the development of Ocean Pines in 1968. Located in Northern Worcester, Ocean Pines is a private residential community featuring nine miles of waterfront property and an array of amenities. Mumfords Landing Yacht Club was named in honor of Zaidee Mumford, whose family sold a large amount of property to Boise Cascade for the Pines development. The yacht club, with its first- and second-story porches, has been surrounded by new structures and is barely visible on the left under the sign. (Historical image courtesy Ocean Pines Association.)

What a difference 40 years makes. Ocean Pines Plaza was developed in the early 1970s to provide gas, food, and retail shopping to the burgeoning Ocean Pines population. Today Ocean Pines has over 10,000 full-time residents, hundreds of summer visitors, and a number of growing neighborhoods nearby. Retail growth here keeps pace with the ever-increasing demand for products and services. (Historical image courtesy Ocean Pines Association.)

Pictured above around 1881, the George Payne house is located on historic West Federal Street in Snow Hill. The homes "fish scale" slate roof, gables, and intricate trim are indicative of Gothic Revival–style architecture. The front porch was modified and a Colonial Revival–style conservatory was added in the early 1900s, but many of the homes original design elements remain. (Historical image courtesy Worcester County Library, Snow Hill Branch.)

Ephraim King Wilson II was a prominent Worcester County attorney who was elected to the US Senate in 1884. This Italianate-style gem was built on West Federal Street in the 1880s for his son William Sydney Wilson. The Hargis family of Snow Hill purchased the home in 1925, and in later years it was converted into apartments. A fire in 2005 caused extensive damage to the interior. (Historical image courtesy Worcester County Library, Snow Hill Branch.)

Constructed in 1930, this building served as a school for elementary and high school students in Snow Hill (notice the school buses parked beside the building in the early image). The sprawling brick structure, one of three identical schools constructed at the same time in Worcester and the only one still standing, is located on South Church Street. The building has been modified and is now an apartment house for senior citizens called Pleasant Manor. (Historical image courtesy Julia A. Purnell Museum.)

Local lawyer Walter P. Snow built this beautiful home in Snow Hill in 1850. The Federal Street residence known as The Cedars has been owned by the Glascox family since 1999 and has been lovingly maintained. In 2007, The Cedars opened as a bed-and-breakfast featuring elegantly appointed historical rooms, many with original light fixtures and horsehair plaster walls. (Historical image courtesy CR Booksellers.)

The Charles Rackliffe House, built in the 1740s near Worcester's Sinepuxent Bay, had become a dilapidated eyesore. The unique Colonial-style plantation home had fallen victim to the elements, the effects of two fires, and extended vacancy; it seemed that razing would be its fate. In 2006, Berlin's Tom Patton, known for his devotion to preserving local history, spearheaded a fight to save the unique home. Under the auspices of Rackliffe House Trust, the property has been leased from the Maryland Department of Natural Resources and magnificently restored. (Historical image courtesy Tom Patton.)

CHAPTER 2

WORKING IN WORCESTER

The fertile, level land in Worcester has always been conducive to farming. Tobacco was an early crop that was followed by corn, wheat, and soybeans. This 1911 image shows Charles Whittington Jones and crew threshing wheat at the Jones Farm on Little Mill Road near Stockton. The farm is still owned and operated by the Jones family. (Courtesy Robert F. Jones, W. Frank Jones Collection.)

On the National Register of Historic Places since 1975, the Iron Furnace in Nassawango is the oldest surviving hot-blast furnace in the country. The Maryland Iron Company built the furnace in 1828, and bog iron was smelted here until its closure in 1847. The dilapidated furnace site was acquired by the Worcester County Historical Society in 1962 and is now maintained by Furnace Town Foundation, Inc. Visitors to the reclaimed furnace and surrounding gardens and shops are afforded a unique look at village life in the mid-1800s. (Historical image courtesy Costen House Museum.)

The busy Ashburn, Child, and King Lumberyard was located near the river in Pocomoke City. The only man identified in this 1910 image is Quince Ashburn (second from the left in the dark suit and light-colored cap). The growth of industry and population in Worcester County in the early 1900s created a big demand for construction materials, and local mills thrived. The business, now in a different location in Pocomoke City, is still family owned and operated. Norma Miles, coauthor of this book and granddaughter of Ashburn, stands at the site of the early warehouse. (Historical image courtesy Costen House Museum.)

Pocomoke City's post office was forced to relocate after a devastating fire in 1922 destroyed its Market Street location. The Peninsula Building, a handsome three-story brick structure located on Front Street, survived the fire unscathed and was able to accommodate the post office and some other displaced businesses. Thanks to the Works Progress Administration, a new post office was built on Market Street in 1937. The Peninsula Building, a landmark near the Pocomoke River since its construction in 1902, was torn down in 1964. (Historical image courtesy Costen House Museum.)

One can only guess as to the exact location of Ocean City's post office in 1912. These simple wooden buildings were likely ruined by one of the many storms that have battered the coastal town and made some early sites unrecognizable. A 1933 hurricane destroyed the town's railroad bridge, and the wind and pounding waves resulted in an inlet being carved between the ocean and the bay. Some locals say the early post office was on Baltimore Avenue; this current picture shows a probable location. (Historical image courtesy Worcester County Library, Snow Hill Branch.)

Snow Hill was founded in 1686 and is the county seat of Worcester County. Major fires, the last in 1893, destroyed many of the town's early buildings, but most of those constructed in the late 19th century to replace them remain in use today. The corner of Pearl and Market Streets, part of the town's historic district, features this beautiful brick building constructed in the early 1900s. The decorative arches over the doors are gone now, but two-toned "eyebrow" trim remains over the windows and a "ghost sign," remnant of some early advertisement, can still be seen on the brick wall facing Pearl Street. This picture, most likely taken in the early 1950s, shows Snow Hill's post office before it relocated to its new home on Washington Street in 1956. An office dedicated to local tourism now occupies this space. (Historical image courtesy Worcester County Library, Snow Hill Branch.)

This is an early 1900s view of Pocomoke City's Market Street looking south. A sign on the left pronounces R.J. Lamden's as "Pocomoke's only Shoe Store." H.W. Callahan's, on the right, advertises "Clothing and Shoes." Horse and carriage was still the transportation of choice, but the rear of an early automobile can be seen at a distance in the middle of the street. The devastating fire of 1922 dramatically changed the face of Market Street; nearly every structure visible in this early image was destroyed. These days the street is lined with pear trees, and visitors to the shops and offices have Market Street bustling again. (Historical image courtesy Worcester County Library, Pocomoke Branch.)

Constructed on the corner of Market Street and Clarke Avenue in Pocomoke City following the 1922 fire, the Veasey Building extended the length of the block to Vine Street and was billed as "the peninsula's largest and best store." The *T*-shaped, two-story building had various retail tenants; Daniel's department store was the last, surviving until the building was razed in 1976. A small park now occupies the site. (Historical image courtesy Winnie Small.)

The facade of the Pocomoke City National Bank building was all that remained after the 1922 fire. The bank found a temporary home at Clogg's Garage, located a few blocks north near the end of Market Street. The bank building was reconstructed on its original site; several banks occupied the space through the years, including Maryland National and, most recently, Calvin B. Taylor Bank. The building, shaded by a massive pear tree, is now home to Pocomoke City Chamber of Commerce. (Historical image courtesy Winnie Small.)

The small brick bank building on Langmaid Road in Newark is empty now, a victim of consolidation. The Home Bank, acquired by Peninsula Bank in the late 1990s and later by PNC (Pittsburgh-Provident National Corporation), received its charter in 1918. The building itself has remained relatively unchanged through the years; some modern lighting and signage was added and what appear to be two plaques flanking the front door have been removed, leaving ghostly imprints behind. The Texaco service station, visible on the left in the 1930s image, is gone now. (Historical image courtesy Julia A. Purnell Museum.)

Girdletree is a small Worcester County village located six miles south of Snow Hill. Local merchant George Barnes constructed a brick bank building here in 1902. The Girdletree Barnes Bank served area customers until it was shuttered in the 1930s. Through the efforts of a local citizen's group, the bank building was restored in 1999 and now operates as a museum. (Historical image courtesy Sandra Hudson.)

Located on Bank Street in Snow Hill, the municipal building has not changed much since its construction in the late 1800s; the sign over the door reads, "1894 MUNICIPAL BUILDING 1908." The large arched doorway, necessary to accommodate the engine when the fire company was located here, has been modified. The two smaller arched doors on the left and right have been replaced with windows. Snow Hill town offices now occupy the building. (Historical image courtesy Worcester County Library, Snow Hill Branch.)

The Worcester County Courthouse was built in 1894 and is located on West Market Street in Snow Hill. Fires destroyed two previous courthouse buildings on this site—first in 1834 and again in 1893. Famed Baltimore architect Jackson C. Gott (1829–1909) designed the redbrick building, and subsequent additions have maintained its handsome, late-19th-century appearance. (Historical image courtesy Julia A. Purnell Museum.)

The Queponco Railway Station on Patey Woods Road in Newark was built in 1910. The station, considered a halfway point between Snow Hill and Berlin, made passenger travel possible in this rural part of Worcester. As roads improved and car travel became a better option, the demand for local trains decreased, and the station stopped serving passengers in the 1960s. The Pennsylvania Railroad, no longer wanting or needing the building, sold it for use as a storage shed. Queponco Railway Station, Inc., a group of local citizens wishing to preserve the history of the old railway station and celebrate its importance to the town of Newark, acquired the building in 1991. The station building has been restored and now functions as the small Queponco Railway Station Museum. (Historical image courtesy Worcester County Library, Snow Hill Branch.)

Pocomoke City's Medieval Revival–style National Guard Armory on Second Street was built in 1927. The local National Guard unit was dissolved in 1968, but the armory building has been put to good use. The large gymnasium has served as a recreation center, and local organizations and the town's civic council have used the office spaces. The Pocomoke City Police Department has been located here since the 1970s. (Historical image courtesy CR Booksellers.)

Horace and Virginia Harmonson built the Atlantic Hotel in 1895 on Berlin's busy Main Street. Vacationers stopped to enjoy food and accommodations on their way to the seaside. Salesmen with calls to make appreciated the adjacent livery stable. A boxy addition in 1946 swallowed up the front of the building, leaving the white window cornices and the rooftop sign as reminders of its former countenance. (Historical image courtesy Tracy Chandler-King.)

Ten local businessmen purchased the property in 1986, and a thorough restoration ensued. Their hard work resulted in a state preservation award from the Maryland Historical Trust in 1989. Today the Atlantic offers 16 sumptuous guest rooms, fine dining, and a location just as desirable as it was over 100 years ago. In 2001, Disney Studios took advantage of the vibe on this section of Main Street by filming much of the movie *Tuck Everlasting* here. The street, thanks to some redressing of the shops and storefronts and several loads of dirt to cover the pavement, easily filled in for the fictional town Treegap around 1910. The building with the second-story porch houses Rayne's Reef Luncheonette, a presence on Main Street since 1901. (Historical image courtesy Mike Queen.)

Snow Hill's Hotel Purnell was built on the corner of Washington and Green Streets in 1894 with Thomas Purnell as the proprietor. A year earlier, fire destroyed the Washington House Tavern at this location. The aforementioned architect Jackson C. Gott designed the comely three-story brick hotel with 22 rooms, a dining area, and a livery stable for the convenience of guests. The hotel was torn down in the 1960s but, except for a few cosmetic changes, this business district has retained its historic flavor. (Historical image courtesy Chris Miles, 1946.)

The Worcester County locality known as Beaverdam lies just north of the Virginia border. In the 1930s, Brantley Watkins ran a rest stop here offering Texaco gas, food, and cabin-style accommodations to travelers along Route 13. In 1950, Watkins built the Twin Tower Motel on this site, featuring every modern convenience, a renowned Chinese American restaurant, and distinctive glass-block towers flanking the front. The Watkins family sold the motel in 1971. The towers are gone now, but lodging is still offered here by Travelers Budget Inn. (Historical image courtesy Bill and Kate Matthews.)

The Ocean City Coast Guard Station has been located on South Philadelphia Avenue since 1964 and has not changed much in appearance. Printed information about the local Coast Guard unit proclaims, "The Coast Guard Stations' primary missions are Search and Rescue and Law Enforcement. In the summer season the tempo of operations increases but in winter it slows considerably." Known as the US Life-Saving Service prior to a merger with the Revenue Cutter Service in 1915, the guardians of Ocean City's coast occupied a structure on Caroline Street as early as 1891. This early Life-Saving Station, carefully preserved, was moved to the inlet area and opened as a local history museum in 1977. (Historical image courtesy CR Booksellers, 1965.)

CHAPTER 3

Schools in Worcester County

This one-room schoolhouse was located on Brantley Road in Pocomoke City. Built around 1900 on land owned by William Sturgis, the school served African American students until the 1940s. In 1991, a group of preservation-minded citizens, together with the Worcester County Historical Society, purchased the ramshackle building from the Sturgis family. It was moved to a downtown site and has been authentically restored and furnished. The Sturgis One Room School is now a museum. (Courtesy Sturgis One Room School Museum.)

Pocomoke City's original high school was built on the corner of Fourth and Walnut Streets in 1867. The handsome two-story building, here hosting a gathering of students in the adjacent schoolyard in the early 1900s (principal Clarke Fontaine is standing at the far left), was torn down in the 1940s. A primary school built on the site served first and second graders for several years, and that building, recently refurbished, is now an activity center for local senior citizens and home to a branch of the Worcester County Health Department. (Historical image courtesy Worcester County Library, Snow Hill Branch.)

Pocomoke City's high school, located on Market Street, was one of eight schools built in Worcester County in 1930. In 1957, a new high school opened on Old Virginia Road, and this building was used for elementary grades. A fire destroyed the aging building in 1972, forcing displaced students to relocate to the newly completed Pocomoke Middle School on nearby Eighth Street. Hartley Hall Nursing Home opened its new facility at this address in 1979. (Historical image courtesy Chris Miles.)

This is the high school built in 1957 on Old Virginia Road to replace the one on Market Street. From left to right, Jennifer (Gladding) Denston, Heidi (Lord) Butler, and Laura (Bloxom) Beauchamp pose near the entrance to Pocomoke High School in 1974. They were photographed again 36 years later while admiring the renovation of their alma mater. The school occupies 32.5 acres and currently serves 480 students in grades 9 through 12. (Historical image courtesy J. Chandler.)

Does this building look familiar? Berlin's Buckingham High School on South Main Street was one of three identical school buildings to open on September 6, 1930, in Worcester County; the other two were located in Snow Hill and Pocomoke City. Stephen Decatur High School, named to honor Worcester County native and war hero Commodore Stephen Decatur, opened nearby in 1954, but Buckingham remained in use as an elementary school until 1978. When the building was razed, the cupola was spared and now sits near the entrance to the current Buckingham Elementary School located at the same site. (Historical image courtesy Taylor House Museum.)

This distinctive domed building in Ocean City was built by the State of Maryland in 1914 for use as a summer institute for teachers. The state allowed the building to be used as a school for many years and finally sold it to Worcester County in 1954. Large trees shade the front of the building now, and there has certainly been some modernization, but most of the unique characteristics of the structure remain. Located on Baltimore Avenue and Third Street just a few blocks from the ocean, this resilient landmark has served as Ocean City's city hall since 1967. (Historical image courtesy Mabel Midgett Rogers.)

From left to right, W. Frank Jones, his wife Esther, and their daughter Helen are pictured on the steps of Stockton's Jones Schoolhouse in 1911. Jones actually took this picture; a close examination will reveal the string he used to operate the camera at a distance. His grandfather Isaac Jones (1808–1859) is reputed to have been a schoolmaster here. The building remained in use as a school until around 1915; it was eventually moved to nearby Goodwill and converted into a dwelling. Robert Jones, a resident of Stockton and a member of the pictured family, stands at the former schoolhouse site. (Historical image courtesy Robert F. Jones, W. Frank Jones Collection.)

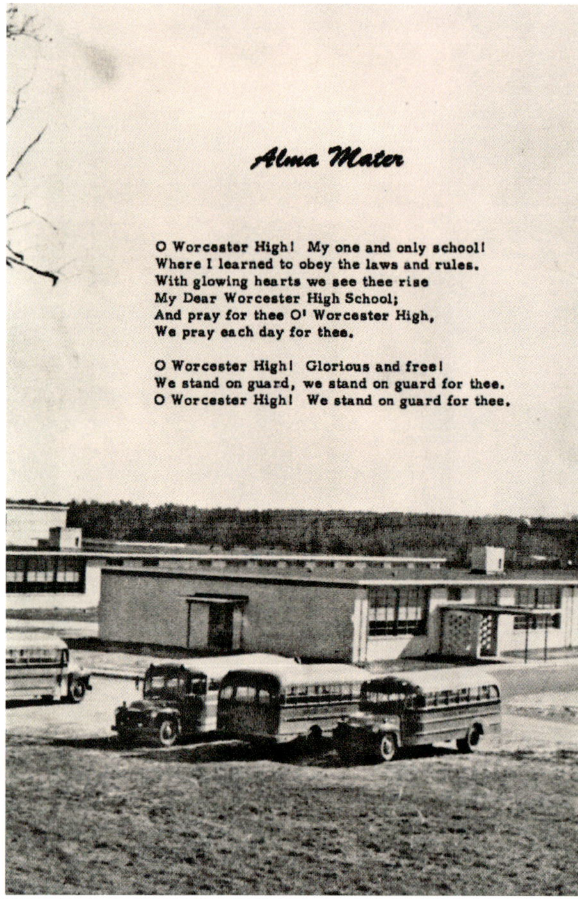

Segregated Worcester Jr. and Sr. High School opened in Newark in 1953; its predecessor, located on Ross Street in nearby Snow Hill, had been graduating African American students since 1937. County schools were fully integrated by 1970, and Worcester High closed. The school buildings are still standing and have been incorporated into the Worcester County Board of Education office complex. (Historical image courtesy Hattie Beckwith.)

CHAPTER 4

Worshiping in Worcester

Little Union Methodist Episcopal Church served African American churchgoers in the rural Worcester County community of Unionville. Some members would cross the Pocomoke River by boat from nearby Puncheon Landing to attend Sunday services. Rev. C.A. Tindley, an esteemed musician, scholar, and Methodist Minister, was the pastor here in the 1890s. By 1892, a new church, Trinity, was completed in Unionville with labor provided by church members. Lorenzo Waters (far right) his wife, Annie (second from right), and three children pose in front of Little Union M.E. Church in this early photograph. (Courtesy Sturgis One Room School Museum.)

Bethany Methodist Church in Pocomoke City was organized in 1832 and has been located on Market Street since 1882. The post office (right) has been its neighbor since 1937. The landscape changed forever on March 3, 2005, when fire completely destroyed the distinctive, Greek-style church building. By the summer of 2007, a new Bethany Methodist Church, thoroughly modern and with a lofty steeple, had been completed on the same site. (Historical image courtesy Worcester County Library, Snow Hill Branch.)

All Hallows Episcopal Church, located on Market Street in Snow Hill, dates to 1748. It is constructed of bricks imported from England and features massive arched doors and windows. A recessed chancel was added in 1891, clear window glass was replaced with stained glass in 1899, and an appropriately styled parish hall was added in 1956. It is easy to imagine colonial-era parishioners arriving here by horse and carriage, dressed in their finest bonnets and breeches. All Hallows has been recognized on the National Register of Historical Places since 1979. (Historical image courtesy Costen House Museum.)

Methodists in Snow Hill first met to worship at a building on Franklin Street. A new building was constructed on Washington Street in 1901 at a cost of $17,000. The church was eventually named to honor L.W. Bates, a well-loved clergyman who served the congregation in 1840 and again in 1858. Bates Memorial Methodist Church underwent a $65,000 renovation in 1947 and has changed very little in the ensuing 60 years. (Historical image courtesy Costen House Museum.)

Formerly St. Agnes Catholic Church, this cottage-style building on Market Street in Snow Hill has been home to the Julia A. Purnell Museum since 1957. Julia A. Purnell (1843–1943) was a prolific needle artist, and her crafts, as well as local history treasures and the work of other artisans, continue to be displayed here. The building, constructed in 1891 to accommodate the town's small Catholic population, had fewer than 20 communicants when it ceased to operate as a church around 1900. (Historical image courtesy Julia A. Purnell Museum, 1968.)

Berlin's Buckingham Presbyterian Church has had a house of worship on South Main Street since the late 1800s; previous meetinghouses at other locations date to 1683. The original church building on this site was destroyed by fire in 1904. This beautiful granite sanctuary was built in 1906, and an annex was added in 1953. (Historical image courtesy CR Booksellers, 1908.)

John Kurtz was quoted in the minutes from a meeting at Snow Hill Mennonite Church in 1954: "The building is a 32 foot by 48 foot cement block structure with a basement, inside lavatories, classrooms and central heat, located two and one half miles north of Snow Hill on a plot of land of the Samuel Yoder farm. The building cost, including landscaping, was $8,855.61. The dedication service was held on October 19th, 1953." Snow Hill Mennonite Church continues to maintain a school and an active congregation. (Historical image courtesy Mary and Maynard Hostetler.)

St. Martin's Episcopal Church, located in Showell, was built in 1756 and served as Worcester's first parish church. In 1954, The Reverend James Trimble Marshall II recounted: "History reveals that after the trying time of the Revolutionary War, the population shifted toward the nearby settlement of Berlin and the old Church was given up as a regular place of worship. St. Martin's was used for a Church School of the Parish for the children in the Showell neighborhood, and it was used as a Methodist Chapel at one time." (Historical image courtesy St. Martin's Church Foundation, Inc.)

A restoration project undertaken in 1994 retained almost all of the structure's colonial features, including the decorative Flemish bond brick walls, box pews, raised pulpit, and original brick floor. St. Martin's Church, added to the National Register of Historical Places in 1977, now functions as a museum and is available to host special events. (Historical image courtesy St. Martin's Church Foundation, Inc.)

St. Paul's Episcopal Church was built in Berlin in 1825 on what is now Church Street. In 1904, fire swept through the town, and at St. Paul's all but the Bishop's chair, lectern, pulpit, and stout outer walls was lost. In rebuilding, a project that included the surviving brick walls, St. Paul's established a handsome Romanesque appearance with its soaring square tower and steep roof gable. The church reopened for worship in 1907 and continues to maintain a thriving parish. Subsequent additions to the building, a parish house in 1908 and Sunday school classrooms in the 1940s, were designed in a complementary style. (Historical image courtesy Costen House Museum.)

Ocean City's Methodists lobbied for a local house of worship in 1915. In 1919, First Methodist Episcopal Church of Ocean City was built on Fourth Street on a lot purchased for $2,000. Additional facilities built here through the years include a parsonage in 1929 and a kitchen and social hall in 1951. In 1962, plans were formed for a new and decidedly modern church building. Contractor A. Hinsel Fink oversaw the construction, and the project was completed in June 1963. First Methodist Episcopal Church of Ocean City, called Atlantic Methodist Church since 1939, became Atlantic United Methodist Church in 1968 following a merger with the Evangelical United Brethren Church. (Historical image courtesy J. Chandler.)

Ocean City's St. Mary Star of the Sea Catholic Church was built on Baltimore Avenue in 1877. Increasing attendance by vacationers led to an expansion of the church building and the addition of a rectory in 1905. By the 1950s, there were as many as nine masses being held here on summer Sundays. Holy Savior Catholic Church was built on Eighteenth Street in 1954 to meet the increasing needs of the parish. Rev. Stephen Connell spearheaded a restoration of St. Mary's in 1974, and work was completed in time to celebrate the church's 100th anniversary in 1977. (Historical image courtesy Mabel Midgett Rogers.)

Built on Philadelphia Avenue and Eighteenth Street in 1954, this is Holy Savior Catholic Church. Adjoining parcels of land were donated to the parish, and in 1968 a 10,000-square foot addition was made to the building. The church looks very different now; the once-austere front now features a lovely colonnade, and a spire has replaced the bell tower. In 2008, the Father Stephen Connell Parish Center, named to honor the dedicated priest who guided the growth of both Ocean City Catholic Churches, opened adjacent to Holy Savior. The sanctuary here can accommodate 1,300 communicants. (Historical image courtesy CR Booksellers, 1957.)

The Church of St. Mary The Virgin on Church Street (now called Third Street) in Pocomoke City was recognized by the local Episcopal diocese in 1855 but had been open for worship 10 years earlier. Rev. Dr. John Crosdale was the church's first full-time rector. He served for 23 years and is buried close to the entrance of the church. St. Mary's exterior appearance has changed very little since the church was enlarged and a bell tower was added in the 1880s. In 1925, fire ravaged the sanctuary, and a full restoration of the interior was necessary. A new social hall, located across the street from the church building, was added in the 1950s, and a child care center opened in recent years. (Historical image courtesy Costen House Museum.)

CHAPTER 5

WORCESTER COUNTY AT PLAY

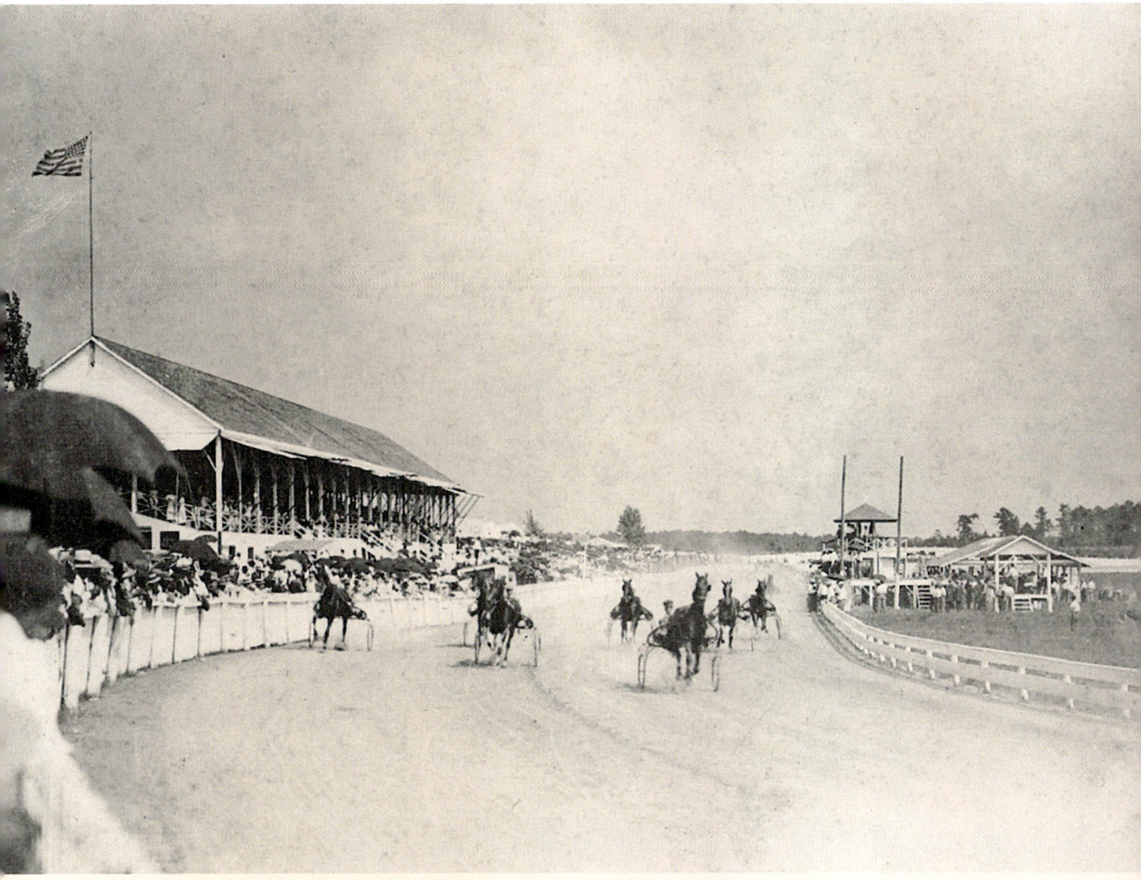

Fairs were a summertime staple in early Worcester County, and the Great Pocomoke Fair, held annually from 1901 through 1930 at the Broad Street Fairgrounds, was one of the largest. Fairgoers enjoyed plenty of good food, carnival rides, and entertainment, as well as the opportunity to watch horse racing from the comfort of a fine grandstand. The stable facilities and racetrack continued to be used by local horsemen for many years following the fair's demise. Reintroduced here in 1991, the Great Pocomoke Fair is once again bringing folks together from far and wide for some late summer fun. (Courtesy Robert F. Jones, W. Frank Jones Collection.)

Fairs have always presented a great opportunity to show off scrumptious cakes and pies, piles of colorful quilts, and garden-fresh produce by the peck full. The chance to show and view blue ribbon–quality livestock is enjoyed at Pocomoke City's annual fair just as much today as it was in the 1920s. (Historical image courtesy Worcester County Library, Pocomoke City Branch.)

The Pocomoke River is 73 miles long and has an average depth of 15 feet. Exploring the river and the swampy wetlands that frame it is a popular pastime for Worcester County's outdoor enthusiasts. Milburn Landing, located on the river near Snow Hill, has been providing camping, boating, and picnicking facilities for over half a century. (Historical image courtesy J. Chandler.)

Shad Landing is another Worcester County recreation area located on the Pocomoke River near Snow Hill. Shad, reached by Route 113, features a campground and access to the river for boaters and fishermen. Campers can also rent canoes, take a dip in the pool, or grab a treat at the snack bar. This state park has been welcoming visitors for over 50 years. (Historical image courtesy J. Chandler.)

Pocomoke City's drawbridge over the river was completed in 1921. This 1930s view shows the waterfront lined with shanties and the keeper's tower clearly visible on the left. In 1988, a section of the drawbridge collapsed into the river; it was rebuilt and opened to traffic in less than a year. These days the bridge area is a haven for pleasure boaters and visitors to Cypress Park, an eight-acre recreation area bordering the Pocomoke River. (Historical image courtesy Costen House Museum.)

Public Landing, a picturesque community located six miles east of Snow Hill on Chincoteague Bay, was an entertainment destination for locals in the 1920s. Visitors could enjoy dancing, bowling, and other amusements in the pier-side buildings. A 24-foot-high waterslide was built adjacent to the pier in 1928. A storm destroyed the waterfront attractions in 1933, and Public Landing became primarily a residential area with access to the bay for crabbing, fishing, and boating. (Historical image courtesy Worcester County Library, Snow Hill Branch.)

Howdy, partner! FrontierTown, a western-themed campground near Ocean City, has been welcoming visitors since 1959. The camping facilities were originally set up to house the many performers who took part in the Wild West shows here, and campsites were made available to guests in 1969. Frontier Town now offers over 500 campsites, a water park, visitor's center, and plenty of amenities. Y'all come! (Historical image courtesy J. Chandler, 1969.)

The art deco–style Mar-Va Theater opened on Market Street in Pocomoke City in 1927. The theater staged vaudeville and minstrel shows and showed movies for 70 years. Deterioration of the building and decreased attendance brought down the final curtain in 1997. Thanks to grants and fund-raisers, a tireless citizen's group was able to purchase and meticulously restore the theater. The Mar-Va, recognized by the National Register of Historic Places in 1996, now shows movies again and serves as a performing arts center. In 2010, a dinner theater production of Neil Simon's *Star-Spangled Girl* was a big hit with theatergoers. (Historical image courtesy Winnie Small, 1955; modern image courtesy Dr. Arnold Torres, 2010.)

Located on Washington Street in Snow Hill, Mason's Opera House was built by Steven Mason in 1908. The 500-seat theater was on the second floor of the distinctive building with various shops occupying the first floor. The third floor was removed prior to 1950, and the building was renovated. It was home to a movie theater, The Outten, for several years and then to a series of retail stores. The old opera house, easily identified by its row of nine windows across the front on the second story, sits empty now. (Historical image courtesy Julia A. Purnell Museum.)

The building that houses the Globe Theater on Broad Street in Berlin was built in 1910 for use as a garage. Frank Bartlett purchased it in 1912 and repurposed it as the area's first movie theater. The structure in Berlin's historic downtown has been utilized in many ways through the years and is now a full-service restaurant and one of Worcester County's most laudable live music venues. (Historical image courtesy Worcester County Library, Snow Hill Branch.)

When this building was completed in 1970, it was called the State Convention Hall. Located from Fortieth to Forty-first Street on Coastal Highway in Ocean City, the convention hall soon became a favorite location to host events of all kinds. The building, extensively enlarged and remodeled in 1997, was renamed the Roland E. Powell Convention Center to honor the much-loved Ocean City mayor. Mayor Powell served the resort town from 1986 until 1996. (Historical image courtesy J. Chandler, 1970.)

The Glen Riddle Farm in Berlin was the home of Samuel D. Ritter and his world-famous racehorses Man O' War and War Admiral. War Admiral was a Triple Crown winner but is best remembered for a race he did not win; he lost what was billed as "The Race of the Century" to the upstart Seabiscuit in 1938. Riddle Farm is now a tony residential development with a world-class golf course. The former stables have been preserved and repurposed; this one is now a restaurant. (Historical image courtesy Taylor House Museum.)

Assateague Island, located near West Ocean City at the end of Maryland Route 611, was designated a National Seashore and State Park in 1962. No one lives on the barrier island; it is a paradise for campers and day-trippers, a habitat for wildlife, and home to the herd of wild ponies made famous by Marguerite Henry's book *Misty of Chincoteague* (a portion of the 37-mile-long island is in Virginia). Assateague was accessible only by boat or ferry across Sinepuxent Bay until 1964. The Verrazano Bridge now connects the island to the mainland with two bridge spans to accommodate automobile and foot traffic. (Historical image courtesy Worcester County Library, Snow Hill Branch.)

Ocean Downs Raceway brought live harness racing to Worcester County in 1949. Located on Racetrack Road in Berlin, the half-mile racetrack, grandstand, and adjacent buildings occupy 170 acres. Thousands of vacationers (Ocean City is just six miles away) and locals alike have flocked to the track each summer for its three-month racing meet. A luxurious clubhouse opened next to the grandstand in 1981, and in 2001 a new restaurant and video wall were added. (Historical image courtesy J. Chandler.)

The stable area at Ocean Downs, the long and narrow buildings clearly visible at left and center in the aerial view of the racetrack grounds, is being readied for demolition at this writing. The facility, already making simulcast viewing and wagering available from 60 racetracks, is preparing to add 800 casino-style slot machines. The property is currently being completely renovated. (Historical image courtesy J. Chandler.)

Worcester County's farmers' markets bring the summer's succulent bounty from local gardens to area tables. Markets can be found in Berlin, Ocean City, Snow Hill, and Pocomoke City. In Pocomoke City, vendors set up on the riverside lots on Front Street, once occupied by the Pocomoke City Garage and the Peninsula Building. The Peninsula Building (right) was demolished in 1964, and the garage was taken down several years earlier. (Historical image courtesy George S. Bunting.)

Ocean City, originally called "Ladies Resort to the Ocean," opened its first hotel in 1875. Now, on summer weekends, as many as 350,000 visitors stay at Worcester's beach resort. These views from the fishing pier show the amazing growth along the nine-mile coastal corridor as a proliferation of businesses, hotels, and condominiums creep toward the Delaware border. (Historical image courtesy CR Booksellers.)

Ocean City's Atlantic Hotel, built between Somerset and Wicomico Streets facing the ocean, was the resort's first hotel and opened to vacationers on July 4, 1875. A fire in 1925 destroyed the Atlantic, the neighboring Seaside Hotel, and several other structures. Rebuilt in 1926 in a distinctive *H*-shape, the Atlantic Hotel is still a favorite with visitors that features a rooftop deck, a row of shops along the front, and a peerless ocean view. (Historical image courtesy Chris Miles.)

Rosalie Tilghman Shreve built the Plimhimmon Hotel around 1890. It was the third hotel located on Ocean City's beachfront. Named "Plimhimmon" after her family's estate in Oxford, Maryland, the hotel became famous for its generous meals and modern rooms that rented for $2.50 a day. The hotel was purchased by brothers Hale and John Harrison in 1970 and renamed Plim Plaza. This boardwalk landmark is still a favorite with vacationers. (Historical image courtesy CR Booksellers.)

The Commander Hotel opened on Fourteenth Street in Ocean City in 1931. The oceanfront hotel, owned and operated by Minnie Lynch, was the northernmost hotel in Ocean City at the time and the first to feature an elevator. Razed and rebuilt at the same location in 1997, the new Commander Hotel bares no resemblance to its predecessor. The Lynch family still owns and operates this lovely hotel. (Historical image courtesy J. Chandler, *c.* 1965.)

The George Washington Hotel, with its distinctive arched entrance and two-story porch, was located "down the beach" on the boardwalk and Tenth Street in Ocean City. An advertisement from the 1940s touted the hotel's 150 feet of ocean frontage, 200 guest rooms, cocktail lounge, and supper club. The Jackson Casino, a popular dancing and gambling venue, was an early neighbor. The hotel building and surrounding area has been modified several times through the years; a bar and various shops front the hotel now at street level and a Sunsations Beachwear store occupies the casino's old spot. No longer known as the George Washington, the hotel had a brief stint as the Mirage and is now an Americana Hotel. (Historical image courtesy CR Booksellers.)

Building the Santa Maria Motor Hotel in 1956 on Fifteenth Street in Ocean City was considered a risky venture. Focusing coffee shops and other guest services toward the outside of the building for the convenience of those traveling by car was a relatively new concept, and the Santa Maria seemed too far north to appeal to visitors. Promising "the convenience of a motel . . . the comfort and luxury of a hotel," the Santa Maria enjoyed 50 prosperous years near the ocean. A modern Marriott property has replaced the three-story concrete motel. (Historical image courtesy CR Booksellers, *c.* 1965.)

The Francis Scott Key, a motel named to honor the Maryland native and author of "The Star Spangled Banner," was built in West Ocean City in 1953. The Hastings family owned and managed the property that featured a main lodge and additional accommodations in cabins and ranch-style buildings. Kenny Baker and Larry Brasher purchased the property in 1972. In 1976, Baker became sole proprietor of the site. Still owned and operated by members of the Baker family, the inn is now called Francis Scott Key Family Resort and features a 1950s-themed diner, numerous playgrounds, indoor and outdoor swimming pools, and 232 guest rooms. The Harry W. Kelly Memorial Bridge, named to honor a favorite local mayor who served Ocean City for 15 years, crosses Sinupuxent Bay and connects the community of West Ocean City to Ocean City. (Historical image courtesy J. Chandler, 1958.)

This is the southern end of Ocean City's boardwalk. The pier amusements can be seen on the right; many more now than in 1965. Barely visible on the lower left in both photographs is the word "House" from the signage of the ride-through Haunted House, a favorite boardwalk attraction since 1962. The building housed a movie theater, nightclub, and roller rink before becoming a scary landmark with a giant bat hovering above the entrance and cars made to look like coffins. (Historical image courtesy Dawn Chandler-Trader, 1965.)

This is a view of Ocean City's North Division Street at the boardwalk. Edward's 5 And 10 opened here in 1937 to sell supplies and souvenirs to beachgoers. Edwards was renovated in 1989 and has just recently given up some floor space to surfing supply shop Quiet Storm. The 1970 image shows the boardwalk's sightseeing train on the left; from Easter through September, the train traverses the three-mile boardwalk every 20 minutes. (Historical image courtesy J. Chandler.)

Ocean City's pier was built in 1906. The building on the left marks the pier's entrance from the boardwalk. The original structure on this site suffered severe storm damage in 1914, and a fire in 1925 destroyed its replacement. The Pier Ballroom, a large venue suitable for dances and conventions, occupied the space for many years. The building is now home to Ripley's Believe It Or Not! Museum (notice the huge shark that appears to be bursting through the building's second story). Dolle's Popcorn is visible in the center of each image, but the passing of 45 years has changed everything else on this part of the boardwalk. (Historical image courtesy J. Chandler.)

The 45 hand-carved animals and other decorative features of Ocean City's Herschel-Spillman Carousel have been delighting visitors of all ages since 1912. Preservation efforts have kept the carousel, one of the boardwalk's oldest continuously operating attractions, relatively unchanged. It was originally purchased by the Trimper family and is still at home in their amusements building near South Division Street. Robin Chandler-Miles (left) and Norma Miles (center) recently took a ride for old time's sake. It is hard to distinguish their picture from the one taken 50 years earlier. (Historical image courtesy J. Chandler.)